The Easy Peasy Vegan Cookbook

Delicious / Healthy / Easy

Appetizers / Soups / Entrees / Desserts

Vegan Recipes For All Occasions

Kathy Jenkins

Copyright ©

All rights reserved. No part of this book may be reproduced, stored in a retrieval system, or transmitted in any form or by any means, electronic, mechanical, photocopying, recording, scanning, or otherwise, without the prior written permission of the publisher.

Disclaimer

All the material contained in this book is provided for educational and informational purposes only. No responsibility can be taken for any results or outcomes resulting from the use of this material.

While every attempt has been made to provide information that is both accurate and effective, the author does not assume any responsibility for the accuracy or use/misuse of this information.

Introduction

The vegetarian way of eating can be a very healthy style of eating. The rules still apply with healthy eating, you should add variety, balance, and moderation.

A vegetarian is someone who avoids all types of meat, whether it be hamburgers, hotdogs, chicken, or even fish. Vegetarians are also sometimes classified by the type of food they are or aren't willing to eat. For example, Lacto-ovo vegetarians will avoid animal flesh yet they will eat eggs and most dairy products. A Vegan on the other hand, will avoid all food that has any trace of animal origin.

Because they don't eat meet, vegetarians will often wonder how they'll get enough protein. Although you may not realize it, the average American actually consumes more protein than he actually needs. For the lacto-ovo vegetarian, dairy products are an excellent source of protein. Vegans on the other hand, get their protein from nuts, seeds, and soy products.

Along the lines of beans, there are several to choose from, including green or red lentils, peanuts, split peas, pinto, soy, kidney, and many more. Some of them you are already familiar, such as kidney beans in chili, refried beans in Mexican dishes, red beans and rice, and pinto beans. Although some beans taste good as they are, others are available with different flavors to help enhance their taste. Nuts are high in protein, although they deliver a lot more fat than beans, which means you should enjoy them in moderation. By having one cup of cooked beans, you'll get the same amount of protein as eating two ounces of meat!

I hope you enjoy these delicious vegan meals and desserts. I have handpicked these recipes from my personal collection. You can cook great tasting meals fast. A lot of these recipes are beginner friendly and can be made quickly.

TABLE OF CONTENTS

APPETIZERS AND DIPS:

- FRESH SPRING ROLLS 9
- VEGAN CHICKPEA TREAT 11
- SOUR CREAM 13
- PESTO 14
- RANCH DRESSING 15
- BRUSCHETTA 16
- PASTA SALAD 17
- EGG SALAD 19

SOUPS:

- CREAMY POTATO LEEK SOUP 21
- TUMERIC MISO SOUP WITH GINGER, GARLIC, AND TOFU ...23
- MINESTRONE - PASTA AND WHITE BEAN SOUP 25
- MALAYSIAN CURRY LAKSA SOUP 28
- SPICED TOMATO SOUP 31
- SPICED CREAMY BROCCOLI SOUP 34
- CARROT AND GINGER SOUP 36
- TACO SOUP 38

ENTREES:

- Baked Tofu Kale Loaf 41
- Berbere Spiced Jackfruit Tacos 43
- Fettuccini Alfredo with Mushrooms 46
- BBQ Sweet Potato Pizza 49
- Vegetable Fajitas Tortilla Pizza......51
- Potato Pesto Pizza.....................54
- Corn Dogs.............................57
- Cajun Lentil Patties...................59
- Artichoke Risotto......................61
- Zucchini-Broccoli Lasagna 63
- Mexican Pizza..........................66
- Bean Burger............................68
- Mac N Cheese...........................70
- Soy Spaghetti..........................72
- Lentil Burgers.........................74
- Moroccan Stew..........................76
- Chili..................................79
- Spinach and Risotto Stuffed Manicotti......81
- Sloppy Joes............................83
- Jambalaya..............................86
- Spanish Casserole......................88
- Stuffed Bell Peppers...................90
- Shepherd's Pie.........................93

Desserts:

- Apple Crisp……………………………….96
- Dark Chocolate Mousse…………………………….98
- Soft Sugar Cookies………………100
- Brownies……………………………102
- Banana Frosting…………………104
- Whole Wheat Scones………………105
- Chocolate Applesauce Cake…….107
- Chocolate Fruit Balls……………108
- Banana Peanut Butter Brownies…………………………….110
- Mixed Berry Muffins (Fat Free and Low Calorie)……..111
- Whole Wheat Cinnamon Raisin Muffins……………113
- Raisin Rice Pudding……………….115
- Pumpkin Pancakes…………………116
- Chocolate Almond Pudding……118
- Banana Bread………………………119
- Popsicles – Chocolate Peanut Butter Banana ……121
- Pumpkin Bars………………………122
- Coffee Cake (Low Fat)…………124
- Double Chocolate Chip Cookies…..126
- Donuts………………………………128
- Peanut Butter Cookies ………..130

- BANANA MUFFINS 132
- VANILLA CUPCAKES 133
- APPLE CARROT MUFFINS 135
- WHOLE WHEAT ZUCCHINI BANANA MUFFINS 137
- FRUIT BUTTER BARS 139
- CHOCOLATE CUPCAKES 141
- BLUEBERRY BANANA MUFFINS 143
- PUMPKIN OATMEAL COOKIES 145
- BANANA CRUMBLE 147
- FUDGE..149
- BREAKFAST COOKIES 151
- WHOLE WHEAT WAFFLES 152
- OATMEAL PANCAKES 153
- CHOCOLATE CAKE....................155
- PUMPKIN CHOCOLATE CHIP COOKIES......157
- GINGER SNAPS.........................159

Fresh Spring Rolls

Ingredients:

Roll:

Vegetables sliced thin (purple cabbage, carrots, cucumber, lettuce)

1 block of firm tofu sliced into sticks and marinated in soy sauce with 1 clove of garlic and a pinch of stevia

8 pieces of rice paper

Vegetable oil spray

Sauce:

1/2 cup hoisin sauce

2 teaspoon sriracha chili sauce or to taste

1 lemon, juiced

Directions:

- Slice vegetables thin
- Marinate tofu in soy sauce mixture
- Place frying pan over medium heat and coat with vegetable oil spray
- Cook tofu slices with marinade until toasted on both sides
- Mix sauce ingredients in a small bowl
- Soak rice paper in a shallow dish of warm water for a few seconds then place on a plate
- Place 2 pieces of tofu, veggies and lettuce in the middle of the rice paper then fold closed like a burrito, repeat with the remaining ingredients
- Serve with dipping sauce

Serving Size: 2 Wraps

Vegan Chickpea Treat

Ingredients:

1 can chickpeas

1 onion

1 pepper (any color)

1 large can of stewed tomatoes or fresh diced

1/2 small can tomato paste

1 portobello mushroom cap

2 cups fresh spinach

spices/seasonings to taste

Directions:

-Wash & cut up all the veggies (except spinach)

-Drain & rince chickpeas

-Drain some of the liquid from the stewed tomatos

(Add above ingredients to a non stick pan)

-Cook until veggies are almost done, then add half a small can of tomato paste

-Season with whatever you would like, salt, pepper, garlic powder, onion powder, paprika, basil

-In the last minute, add the spinach and stir until it starts to wilt.

-Serve right away.

Number of Servings: 4

Sour Cream

Ingredients:

1 (16 ounce) package silken tofu

1 tablespoon olive oil (or canola)

4 -5 teaspoons lemon juice

2 teaspoons apple cider vinegar

1 teaspoon sugar (or your favorite sweetener)

1/2-1 teaspoon salt, to taste

Directions:

-Place all ingredients in a blender.

-Process five minutes, until very creamy and smooth.

-Refrigerate for at least an hour to thicken.

-Use within 5-6 days.

Number of Servings: Yield 1 ½ cups of sour cream

Vegan Pesto

Ingredients:

12-15 fresh basil leaves

2-3 garlic cloves

1/2 teaspoon course sea salt

1 tablespoon toasted pine nuts

1 tablespoon walnut pieces

1 tablespoon nutritional yeast

3 tablespoons olive oil

Directions:

-Add all ingredients up to the oil to a food processor and process until a puree is formed.

-Drizzle in the oil and pulse a few more times to combine.

Number of Servings: 4

Vegan Ranch Dressing

Ingredients:

1 cup vegan mayonnaise

1/2 teaspoon garlic powder

1/2 teaspoon onion powder

1/4 teaspoon black pepper

2 teaspoons parsley, chopped

1/2 cup unsweetened soymilk

Directions:

-Whisk all ingredients together and chill before serving.

-Add a little more soy milk if you need to thin dressing.

Number of Servings: Yields 2 cups of dressing

Vegan Bruschetta

Ingredients:

2 tomatoes

1/2 teaspoon minced garlic

1 teaspoon balsamic vinegar

8 fresh basil leaves

black pepper - to taste

12 slices (1/2 inch) of a long loaf of Italian bread

Directions:

-Mix all topping ingredients together.

-Spread evenly over each slice of bread.

-Toast until crisp at 375 deg.

Number of Servings: 12

Vegan Pasta Salad

Ingredients:

4 cups whole wheat pasta (cooked)

1/4 cup red wine vinegar

1/4 cup balsamic vinegar

1 tablespoon dijon mustard

1/4 cup extra virgin olive oil

2 cloves of garlic, minced

salt to taste

freshly cracked black pepper to taste

1/4 cup olives

1 small zucchini

scallions (optional for garnish)

Directions:

-Cook pasta according to package directions to yield 4 cups. Drain.

-Drizzle with half the olive oil to keep the pasta from sticking. Set aside.

-Chop olives and zucchini and set aside.

-Combine both vinegars, Dijon mustard, remaining olive oil and garlic and whisk.

-Coat pasta with mixture. Mix in zucchini and olives. Add salt and pepper to taste.

-Top with chopped scallions (optional), cover bowl and refrigerate until ready to serve.

Number of Servings: 4

Vegan Egg Salad

Ingredients:

1 lb firm tofu, frozen and then thawed

1 stalk celery, diced

1/4 medium red onion, chopped

1 small carrot, finely chopped

1/2 cup soy mayonnaise

2 tablespoons soy sauce

1/2 teaspoon lemon juice or vinegar

1/2 - 3/4 teaspoon kelp powder

Directions:

-Thaw tofu, squeeze the excess moisture out and crumble it into small pieces.

-In a medium bowl, combine the tofu, celery, onions, and carrot.

-Stir in the mayonnaise, soy sauce, lemon juice, and kelp and mix together well.

Makes 4 servings

SOUPS

Creamy Potato Leek Soup

Ingredients:

1 tablespoon extra-virgin olive oil

2 leeks, white and light green parts washed and sliced into 1/4-inch slices

2 cups chopped yellow onion

1/2 teaspoon sea salt

3 cloves garlic, minced

2 large potatoes (about 1 pound), peeled and cubed into 1/2-inch cubes

4 cups vegetable stock

2-3 teaspoons fresh rosemary leaves

Directions:

-Heat a 4-quart soup pot over medium heat and add the oil.

-Add the leeks, onion, and sea salt and saute for about 5 minutes, stirring often, until the onion begins to turn translucent.

-Add the garlic and stir well. Cook for 1 minute more.

-Add the potatoes and vegetable stock, cover, and bring to a boil. Reduce heat to simmer. Cook 20 minutes.

-Remove the soup from the heat and use an immersion/stick blender to blend the soup in the pot or ladle the soup into a blender, 1 cup at a time. Blend the soup with the fresh rosemary leaves until smooth and free of chunks. Pour smooth soup into a heat-proof bowl and continue until all of the soup has been blended.

-Transfer the blended soup back to the original soup pot and warm over low heat until heated through. Serve hot.

Number of Servings: 5

Tumeric Miso Soup with Ginger, Garlic, and Tofu

Ingredients:

1 tsp oil

7 cloves of garlic, finely chopped

1 to 1.5 inch piece of ginger, peeled and minced

½ hot green chile (optional)

½ to ¾ cup grated or shredded carrots

½ green or red bell pepper thinly sliced

7 oz (1/2 a block) of tofu, cubed small

2 tsp tamari or soy sauce

2.5 to 3.5 cups water (to preference)

½ tsp or more turmeric

1 tsp apple cider or distilled white vinegar

1 tsp or more sugar or maple syrup

½ tsp salt, less or more to taste, depends on your miso

½ tsp freshly ground black pepper, divided

1 tbsp or more white mellow miso

scallions for garnish

Directions:

Heat oil in saucepan over medium heat. Add garlic, ginger and chile and cook until translucent. 4 mins.

Add the carrots and peppers and cook for 3 minutes.

Add tofu and mix in. At this point you can also add in chopped veggies(chopped small) such broccoli.

Add water, ⅓ tsp black pepper and rest of the ingredients except miso and bring to a boil.

Simmer for 4 minutes. Then add the miso and mix in. Taste and adjust salt, sweet and tang(vinegar). Simmer for another few minutes.

Garnish with scallions and black pepper.

Number of Servings: 2

Vegan Minestrone (Pasta and White Bean Soup)

Ingredients:

1 tsp olive oil

½ cup chopped onion, chopped

4 cloves of garlic, chopped

½ cup chopped celery

¾ cup chopped carrots

1 28 oz can diced tomato

1 15 oz can cannellini beans,or other white beans or a combination of white and kidney beans

1 cup chopped zucchini

3 cups water

½ tsp salt

½ tsp oregano

¼ tsp thyme

¼ tsp black pepper

½ cup elbows or other pasta (use gluten-free if needed)

1 cup baby spinach

3 tbsp chopped basil

Directions:

Heat oil in a large saucepan over medium heat. Add onion and garlic and cook until translucent. 4 mins.

Add celery, carrots and tomato and bring to a boil. 4 to 5 mins.

Add the beans, zucchini, water, salt and spices and cook for 15 to 18 minutes.

Add ½ cup pasta and simmer for 12 or more minutes. Taste and adjust salt, herbs and heat.

Fold in spinach and 2 tbsp chopped basil and simmer for another minute. Serve hot garnished with fresh basil and vegan parmesan.

Number of Servings: 4

Vegan Laksa – Malaysian Curry Laksa Soup

Ingredients:

Laksa Paste:

2 tsp coriander seeds

½ tsp fennel or cumin seeds

1 inch fresh turmeric root, peeled if needed(or use 1 tsp or more ground turmeric)

1 inch fresh ginger root (peeled if needed)

1 green chile

½ tsp cayenne or use paprika + cayenne

1 stalk lemongrass

3 cloves of garlic

2 tbsp raw cashews, soaked for 15 mins, use almonds or pepitas for cashew-free

a good handful of cilantro with tender stems

1 tsp lime juice

Laksa Curry Soup:

1 tsp oil

Laksa curry paste from above

2 cups sliced white mushrooms

¾ cup sliced carrots

½ to 1 cup other veggies of choice (sliced or chopped small), such as bell peppers, zucchini, broccoli etc

3 cups veggie broth or water

1 13.5 oz can coconut milk, about 1.5 cups

6 to 8 oz brown rice noodles (uncooked)

1 cup of chopped spinach or chard

salt and cayenne to taste

sugar or sweetener if needed

cilantro, mint for garnish

Directions:

Make the paste:

Toast the coriander and fennel seeds for 2 to 3 minutes or until fragrant. Add to a blender or spice grinder and grind to a coarse mixture.

Add the rest of the ingredients to a blender or food processor and blend until pasty. Add a tbsp or so water if needed. The paste can be refrigerated for up to a week and frozen for longer..

Make the soup:

Heat oil in a saucepan over medium heat. Add all of the curry paste (1/3 to ½ cup) and fry for 3 minutes. Stir occasionally. If using premade paste, use a ⅓ cup.

Add the mushrooms and cook for 2 minutes.

Add the veggies, broth and coconut milk and bring to a boil. Reduce heat to medium low. Add in the rice noodles and let the mixture simmer for 10 minutes.

Fold in the spinach and chard. Taste and adjust salt and heat. I usually add a bit of salt or soy sauce, lime juice and some sugar at this point. Add more coconut milk if needed. Simmer for another few minutes. Garnish with fresh cilantro, mint, bean sprouts or crisped tofu and serve.

Spiced Tomato Soup Recipe

Ingredients:

½ tsp oil

¼ tsp cumin seeds

½ cup chopped onion

3 cloves of garlic

¼ cup chopped carrot, or 1 medium carrot, chopped

½ tsp ground coriander

¼ tsp turmeric

¼ tsp cayenne

¼ tsp black pepper or a combination of black and white pepper

1 15 oz can tomatoes

1 cup water

½ tsp salt

1½ to 2 tsp sugar

1 small bay leaf

Directions:

Heat oil in a saucepan over medium heat. When hot, add cumin and cook for 1 minute or until the cumin seeds get fragrant.

Add chopped onions, garlic, carrot and a pinch of salt. Cook for 4 to 5 minutes or until onions are translucent. Stir occasionally.

Add coriander, turmeric, cayenne and pepper, mix for a few seconds.

Add the onion mixture to a blender. Add tomatoes and blend until pureed.

Transfer the pureed tomato mixture back to the saucepan. Add water, bay leaf, salt and sugar and cook over medium heat for 12 to 14 minutes. Taste and adjust salt, sweet and heat. Add more water if needed. Garnish with chives and Serve with crusty bread or croutons or grilled vegan cheese sandwiches.

NOTES

Quick tip, chop the onions, carrot garlic in a processor to save time. Use spices and herbs of choice for variation.

Make it creamy: Add 2 to 3 tbsp cashews or pumpkin seeds or a ¼ cup chickpeas or white beans at step 4.

Make it oil-free: Dry roast the cumin seeds until fragrant, then add the onions, garlic, carrots and a splash or water or veggie broth and continue.

Spiced Creamy Broccoli Soup

Ingredients:

2 tsp extra virgin olive oil

½ cup chopped onion, red, or white

2 cups or more grated broccoli or broccoli slaw

1 tsp garlic powder

¼ tsp onion powder

¼ tsp black pepper

⅓ tsp ground cumin

½ tsp ground coriander

¼ tsp or more cayenne

2 tbsp or more nutritional yeast

¾ tsp or more salt

3 tbsp chopped fresh basil or dried basil to taste

¼ cup cashews, soaked for 15 minutes or longer (1/3 cup for creamier)

2 cups or more non dairy milk, unsweetened

cayenne for garnish

Directions:

Heat oil in a saucepan over medium low heat. Add onions and a dash of salt and cook until mostly translucent. about 6 minutes.

Add the shredded broccoli and spices. Mix and cook for 1 minute. Mix in the nutritional yeast and salt. I used some broccoli stems and some florets and processed them in a food processor to get about 2 cups grated broccoli.

Blend the cashews and basil with 1 cup non dairy milk until smooth. Blend a couple of times if the cashews were not soaked. Add to the saucepan. Add the rest of the non dairy milk and mix in. Bring to a boil. About 5 mins. If the soup starts to thicken too much or needs more liquid. Add ¼ to ½ cup or more water and mix in. Taste and adjust salt and spice.

Simmer for another 3 to 5 minutes or until desired consistency. Garnish with cayenne or red pepper flakes. Serve with warm garlic bread or crackers.

Number of Servings: 2

Vegan Carrot and Ginger Soup

Ingredients:

1 tablespoon olive oil

1 1/2 cups onions (chopped or diced)

2-3 cloves garlic (minced or pressed)

4 cups fresh carrots (chopped or diced)

1 to 1 1/2 teaspoons ginger (freshly grated)

4 cups vegetable broth (or water)

1/4 cup orange juice

3 cups rice milk (or soy milk)

salt and pepper to taste

Directions:

-Sauté' the olive oil, onions and garlic in the bottom of a large pot until the onions are translucent (3-4 minutes). Add the carrots, ginger, and broth.

-Boil until the carrots are very tender (30-35 minutes).

-Puree the mixture in a food processor/blender or mash it in the pot with a potato masher.

-Return the mixture to the stove. Heat until warm.

-Add the orange juice and rice milk. Do not boil!

-Salt and pepper to taste. Serve immediately.

Number of Servings: 6

Vegan Taco Soup

Ingredients:

2 cans of diced tomatoes

3 cups of tomato juice (V8)

1 large jalapeno.

3 cloves garlic.

2 large boxes of veggie broth

4 cans of black beans

2 cans of kidney beans

2 cups cilantro leaves

1 cup sweet onions

½ cup green onions

1 can of green chiles

1 cup canned corn

season to taste

Directions:

-Simple, add all ingredients into pot and cook until hot.

Number of Servings: 10

ENTREES

Baked Tofu Kale Loaf

Ingredients:

2 tablespoons olive oil

1 (14oz) block extra-firm tofu

1 clove garlic (minced)

3 tablespoons ketchup

1 tablespoon dijon mustard

1 tablespoon tamari (or soy sauce)

1 cup kale (finely chopped)

1/4 teaspoon black pepper

1 tablespoon peanut butter

1 cup carrots (thinly sliced)

Directions:

-Preheat oven to 350*F (175*C). Oil a 9 inch loaf pan with the olive oil (leaving some excess in the pan) and set aside.

-Rinse and drain the tofu, squeeze with a few paper towels to remove excess water. Crumble it. Place the crumbled tofu into a large mixing bowl.

-Toss the rest of the ingredients into the bowl and mix well. Pour into the loaf pan, pressing firmly and evenly.

-Bake for 55-60 minutes, let cool for 10 minutes before serving.

Number of Servings: 6

Berbere Spiced Jackfruit Tacos

Ingredients:

20 oz can jackfruit

1 medium onion roughly chopped

8 cloves of garlic , more the merrier

1 tbsp oil , olive or safflower

1/2 tsp salt

Flavoring:

2 tsp or more paprika i use 1 tsp smoked and 1 tsp sweet paprika

2 tsp berbere spice blend , less or more to heat and flavor preferene

1/2 tsp ground cumin

1 tsp ground coriander

1/2 tsp garlic powder

1/4 tsp cinnamon   optional

1/4 tsp or more cayenne if berbere is not hot

1 to 2 tbsp bbq sauce

1 tbsp maple syrup

2 tsp soy sauce or use coconut aminos for soy-free or omit

Directions:

Squeeze the jackfruit in between paper towels to remove as much liquid as possible. It is ok if it squishes.

Process with onion, garlic and jackfruit in a prcessor until coarsely shredded. Alternatively, finely chop the onion and garlic and finely chop/shred the jackfruit.

Transfer to a bowl and mix in the spices and sauces well. Preheat the oven to 350 degrees F.

Spread the mixture on a parchment lined baking sheet so its an even layer.

Bake at 350 degrees F for 35 to 40 minutes. Mix and spread after 20 minutes to move the center portion out. Also taste at this time for salt, heat and flavor. Adjust if needed and mix in.

Prep your tortillas. Add a good helping of the jackfruit mixture. Add cucumbers or other crunchy veggies. Add a creamy dressing like tahini dressing, or vegan ranch dressing or tzaztiki

Number of Servings: 3

Vegan Fettuccini Alfredo with Mushrooms (Nut Free)

Ingredients:

Mushrooms:

1 tsp olive oil

1/2 medium onion chopped

7 cloves garlic minced

8 oz mushrooms white or a mix of white, cremini, portobello

1 tbsp or more dry white wine

1 tbsp vegan worcestershire sauce or use 2 tsp soy sauce (coconut aminos for soyfree), 1/2 tsp apple cider vinegar, 1/2 tsp molasses

1/4 tsp thyme

1/4 tsp or more red pepper flakes

Alfredo:

8 to 10 oz Fettuccine

1 cup cauliflower florets heaping cup of florets

1 small potato cubed small

2 tbsp hemp seeds or pumpkin seeds , or use raw cashews (soaked) for even more creamier

1/4 tsp onion powder

1/4 tsp garlic powder

2 tsp lemon juice

3/4 tsp salt

1/2 tsp dried basil or a handful of fresh

1 tbsp nutritional yeast

1 tbsp extra virgin olive oil

1 cup water

generous dash of black pepper

Directions:

-Heat oil in a large skillet over medium heat. Add onion, garlic, mushrooms and a good pinch of salt and cook until golden. Add the wine, sauce and pepper flakes and cook for half a minute.

-Bring a large wide pot of water to a boil. Add the fettuccine and cook for 3 minutes. Mix. Add the cauliflower and potatoes on top of the pasta and continue to cook for 5 to 6 minutes or until the pasta is cooked to preference. *See note

-Drain, rinse in cold water. Remove the cauliflower and potato and Transfer to the blender.

-Add the rest of the alfredo ingredients to the blender. Add 2 tbsp of the mushroom onion mixture and blend until smooth. Blend for a minute, then rest for a minute and blend again.

-Pour sauce into the mushroom skillet and cook over medium heat to bring to a boil to thicken. Taste and adjust salt and flavor. If the sauce thickens too much, add in some more water or non dairy milk. Mix in the fettuccine and serve. Alternatively, plate the fettuccine and drizzle the sauce generously and serve. Garnish with basil and pepper.

Number of Servings: 3

BBQ Sweet Potato Pizza with Homemade BBQ Seasoning

Ingredients:

1 pizza crust (of your preference)

1 small sweet potato cubed

1/3 cup corn kernels, thawed if frozen

1/2 onion, sliced sliced thick

peppers or other veggies

1 sliced jalapeno

1/3 cup soy-free bbq sauce or other bbq sauce of choice

BBQ Seasoning:

1/2 tsp each of garlic powder oregano/parsley, ground mustard

1/4 tsp each of onion powder thyme, cayenne, salt, celery seed

1 tsp smoked paprika

1 tsp coconut sugar

Directions:

-Boil the Sweet potato and corn in a saucepan over medium heat. Add water just to cover the veggies. Boil for 5 minutes once boiling. Drain and cool for a minute then transfer to a bowl.

-Toss with onions, peppers/veggies and 2 tbsp bbq sauce and a good dash of black pepper.

-Shape the pizza dough into one large thin crust pizza.

-Brush olive oil on the pizza dough. Spread Sweet potato mixture on the pizza. Add jalapeno. Sprinkle bbq seasoning all over the veggies generously. Drizzle some or all of the bbq sauce.

-Bake at 425 degrees for 16 to 18 minutes. Cool for a minute. Garnish with cilantro, more bbq seasoning and more bbq sauce if you wish. Slice and serve.

Number of Servings: 3

Vegetable Fajitas Tortilla Pizza

Ingredients:

Fajita Veggies:

1/2 tsp oil

2 Bell Peppers (1 green and 1 red), thinly sliced

1/2 medium onion, sliced

1/4 tsp salt

1/2 tsp cumin

1 tsp smoked paprika (or use half sweet and half smoked paprika)

1/2 tsp oregano

1/2 tsp garlic powder

1/4 tsp cayenne or chipotle pepper powder

a generous pinch black pepper

a dash of lemon towards the end

1/4 to 1/2 cup corn kernels (thawed if frozen)

1 small zucchini, thinly sliced

Pizza:

vegan mozzarella cheese

pepper flakes and basil for garnish

2 to 4 tortillas

Directions:

Fajita Veggies:

Heat oil in a skillet over medium high heat. When hot, add the peppers, onion and a good pinch of salt. Cook until golden on some sides (4 to 6 minutes). Stir occasionally. Add the spices and mix in.

Add corn, zucchini and salt. Mix and Cook for 2 to 3 minutes. At this time you can add some beans to the skillet as well. Taste and adjust spices, flavor and salt. Add more spices if adding beans or more veggies. Add a dash of lemon and mix.

Pizza:

Spread tomato/pizza sauce or marinara on tortillas. Spread the fajita vegetable mixture from above. Add vegan cheese. Bake at 425 degrees F for 10 mins, or Grill in a covered grill to melt the cheese. Garnish with pepper flakes and basil or shredded lettuce, salsa and other toppings of choice.

Make quesadillas: Spread the sauce and the veggies on half a large tortilla. Add vegan cheese, fold and grill.

Make Tacos: Warm the tortilla. Fill with the fajita vegetables. Add dressing of choice like a Chile Lime dressing. Add shredded lettuce and salsa or guacamole.

Number of Servings: 2

Vegan Potato Pesto Pizza

Ingredients:

Pesto:

1 well packed cup Basil

1 cup loosely packed spinach

2 cloves garlic

2 tbsp extra virgin olive oil

1 tbsp lemon juice

3 tbsp cashews or other nuts such as walnuts, pine nuts

water as needed

¼ tsp salt

Pizza:

1 Recipe 20 Minute Pizza Crust with half Spelt flour and half unbleached white/all purpose

1 large or 2 medium potatoes (yukon or other) thinly Sliced

½ red onion thinly sliced or use leeks

2 cloves of garlic, thinly sliced

1 tbsp extra virgin olive oil

salt and freshly ground black pepper

Directions:

-Make the pesto. Blend everything with 1-2 tbsp of water until the nuts are coarsely blended and the basil is well blended. Alternatively, pulse the nuts in a small blender or processor until a coarse meal, then add the rest of the ingredients and blend or process until well combined.

-Preheat the oven to 425 deg F. Prep your pizza dough. I use half Whole grain Spelt and half unbleached white flour for the pizza dough. Let the dough rest near the warming oven for 10 mins. Divide into 2 balls and roll them out into 2 medium size thin crust pizzas or 1 large thin crust.

-Spread the prepared pesto over the crust.

-Slice the potatoes using a mandolin or a sharp knife. Layer over the pesto.

-Layer sliced onion and garlic, Spray or brush extra virgin olive oil. Sprinkle salt and generous freshly ground pepper. Add some veggie crumbles, vegan coconut bacon or other crisp toppings (optional)

-Bake at 425 degrees F for 17 to 18 mins. Add some crisp greens on top (optional). Cool for a minute. Slice and serve.

Number of Servings: 4

Vegan Corn Dogs

Ingredients:

6 tofu hot dogs or 6 vegetarian hot dogs

6 skewers

1/2 cup yellow cornmeal

1/2 cup flour

1 teaspoon dry mustard

1/2 teaspoon salt

1 egg substitute

1 tablespoon sugar

1 teaspoon baking powder

1/2 cup soymilk

1 tablespoon melted shortening

Directions:

-Combine the cornmeal, flour, sugar, mustard, baking powder and salt. Mix well.

-Add the soymilk, egg replacer and shortening and mix until very smooth.

-Pour this mixture into a tall glass.

-Put the dogs on the sticks and dip them into the cornmeal batter to coat evenly.

-Deep fry in oil heated to 350°F until golden brown, about 2 minutes.

-Drain on paper towels.

Number of Servings: 6

Vegan Cajun Lentil Patties

Ingredients:

2 cups of lentils, cooked according to instructions

1 cup soft tofu

1 medium onion, diced

6 medium mushrooms, diced

1 medium carrot, grated

2 cloves garlic, diced

1 teaspoon cajun seasoning

1/2 teaspoon Italian mixed herbs

salt to taste

freshly ground black pepper to taste

olive oil for frying

Directions:
:

-Fry the mushroom in the olive oil for 5 minutes, stirring regularly.

-Add the grated carrot, onion and garlic and cook for another 5 minutes.

-Add the lentils, tofu, Cajun seasoning and herbs.

-Cook for 10 minutes stirring regularly. The mixture will all clump together.

-Season with salt and freshly grated black pepper.

-Leave to cool. When cool enough to handle shape into small patties.

-Fry in a small amount of olive oil for 5 minutes on each side.

Number of Servings: 6

Vegan Artichoke Risotto

Ingredients:

2 tablespoons olive oil

1 tablespoon unsalted margarine

1 small onion, chopped

2 cups uncooked carnaroli rice

1/4 cup soy milk (or skim milk)

1/4 cup apple juice

6 cups vegetable stock

1 (8 ounce) container firm tofu, cubed

1 (6.5 ounce) jar marinated artichoke hearts, drained, liquid reserved

2 cloves garlic, minced

1 (8.75 ounce) can low salt yellow corn

cayenne pepper to taste

Directions:

-In a large saucepan over medium heat, heat oil and margarine. Stir in 1/2 the onion, and saute until tender. Stir in the rice, and cook until lightly browned.

-Pour soy milk and apple juice into the rice. When the rice has absorbed the liquids, gradually pour in vegetable stock, about 1/2 cup at a time, until absorbed. Reserve about 1/4 cup stock. Cover, and cook about 20 minutes, until rice is tender.

-In a medium saucepan over medium heat, lightly brown the tofu and remaining onion in the reserved marinated artichoke heart liquid. Stir in the garlic.

-Remove the rice from heat, and thoroughly mix remaining vegetable stock, tofu mixture, artichoke hearts, corn, and cayenne pepper into the rice.

Makes 8 servings.

Vegan Zucchini-Broccoli Lasagna

Ingredients:

Sauce:

2 cans crushed tomatoes

1 can tomato sauce

splash of red wine

minced garlic

minced dried onions

dried herbs, salt, and pepper to taste

Filling:

1 head of broccoli

3 medium zucchini

1 large block of soft tofu (firm or extra firm will work too)

Seasonings to taste

Layering:

Flat lasagna noodles (12)

2 bags of shredded mozzarella flavor vegan cheese

Directions:

-Make sauce:

In medium saucepan, combine the sauce ingredients and cook over medium to low heat until reduced by about 1/4.

-Make filling:

Steam broccoli in microwave. Chop finely.

Dice zucchini and saute in nonstick pan sprayed with pam, until tender. Add garlic and saute a bit more. Finally, add the crumbled tofu, and cook all together until much of the water cooks off (about 10-15 minutes). Season to taste.

-Puree veggie/tofu mixture with submersion blender to make creamy, spreadable filling.

-Layer filling, sauce, and vegan cheese shreds with uncooked lasagna noodles. Bake at 350 for 30-40 minutes.

Number of Servings: 8

Vegan Mexican Pizza

Ingredients:

1/4 cup of black beans

1/4 cup of cooked spinach

2 medium flour tortillas

1 teaspoon black pepper

1 oz green chili sauce

1/4 avocado

2 tablespoons salsa

Directions:

-Lay the tortillas out and on one, spread the mashed black beans. On the other tortilla spread the spinach. Make sure to cover them completely. Spread the green chili sauce evenly over the black bean side. Sprinkle the black pepper evenly over the spinach side.

-On a skillet sprayed with pam, place the tortilla side of the black bean half onto it and let it sit for a couple of minutes until it starts to get crisp. Then place the spinach side of the half onto it and let it sit for another minute or so. Then flip

-Let that sit for a few minutes until crispy and lightly golden. When done, place the quesadilla on a plate.

-Next spread the ripe avocado all over the top and spread the salsa evenly over the top

Number of Servings: 1

Vegan Bean Burger Recipe

Ingredients:

2 cans black beans (rinsed and drained)

2 carrots, grated

1/2 cup dry rolled oats

1/4 cup pepitas (pumpkin seeds)

1 tablespoon olive oil

1/2 teaspoon cinnamon

1/2 teaspoon cumin

1/2 teaspoon coriander

1/2 teaspoon chili powder

1/2 teaspoon onion powder

1/4 teaspoon cayenne pepper

1 teaspoon sea salt

1/4 tsp black pepper

Directions:

-Preheat oven to 300 degrees.

-Next, add the oats and pepitas to your food processor and grind until coarsely chopped. Let it run for roughly 10 seconds. Grate the carrots, and then add to your mixture in the food processor. Add 3/4 of the beans, all spices, and the olive oil. Once all of this is in the food processor, mix it all together.

-Spoon mixture into a mixing bowl and then fold in the rest of the whole, reserved beans.

-Wet your hands and then form into 6 medium sized patties. Place patties on a non-stick baking sheet or into a baking pan

-Bake at 300 degrees for 40 minutes, turning once in the middle. If you want to grill these, pre-bake them for 30 minutes at 300, and then throw them on the grill to reheat and get a little extra browning.

Number of Servings: 6

Vegan Mac N Cheese

Ingredients:

1 1/2 cups plain soymilk

1cup water

1/3cup tamari or 1/3 cup soy sauce

1 1/2cups nutritional yeast

1tablespoon paprika

1tablespoon garlic powder

1tablespoon salt

3ounces firm tofu

1cup canola oil

1 1/2lbs macaroni noodles

2teaspoons mustard (optional)

Directions:

-Preheat oven to 350°F.

-Boil water in a big pot for the pasta.

-All of the ingredients sans pasta can easily go in a blender (liquid and powdered) this is by far the easiest way.

-Once pasta is cooked, drain and put it in the baking pan pour the cheese sauce over the pasta.

-Bake until the top of the pasta looks slightly browned and crispy about 15 minutes.

Number of Servings: 6

Vegan Soy Spaghetti

Ingredients:

1 box whole soybean pasta

1 can tomato w/basil & oregano soup

1 package veggie ground beef

1/2 cup chopped mushrooms

3/4 cup chopped bell peppers

1/4 cup chopped onions

Directions:

-Start boiling water for the pasta.

-Put all the veggies in a pan and sauté them until they start to get tender, then add the veggie ground beef.

-Add your pasta when the water starts boiling and cook according to package directions.

-While the pasta is cooking, and the veggies are nearly done, add in the soup and mix, adding water or vegetable broth to get a good sauce consistency.

-Spoon the sauce over the finished pasta and serve.

Number of Servings: 4

Vegan Lentil Burgers

Ingredients:

1 cup uncooked lentils

1 cup uncooked brown rice

1 1/2 cups carrots, finely grated

1/2 teaspoon garlic powder

1 1/2 cups uncooked oatmeal

1 teaspoon season salt

1 small onion, finely grated

Directions:

-Cook lentils and rice in 4 cups water for 45 minutes, simmering over low heat in a covered pan. Allow to cool.

-Add remaining ingredients and mix well.

-Shape into patties and cook on griddle or pan (may spray with non-stick spray) over medium heat, until nicely browned (about 6 minutes per side).

Number of Servings: 8

Vegan Moroccan Stew

Ingredients:

2 teaspoons extra virgin olive oil

1 cup chopped onions

½ cup each diced celery and chopped green bell pepper

2 cloves garlic, minced or sliced thinly

3 cups vegetable broth

3 cups peeled, cubed sweet potatoes

1 can diced tomatoes

1 can chickpeas, drained and rinsed

1 tablespoon lemon juice

2 teaspoons grated ginger root

1 teaspoon each ground cumin, curry powder, ground coriander, and chili powder.

½ teaspoon ground pepper

¼ cup raisins

2 tablespoons each natural peanut butter and chopped, fresh cilantro

Directions:

-Heat olive oil in a large, non-stick saucepan over medium-high heat. Add onions, celery, green pepper, and garlic. Cook and stir until vegetables begin to soften, about 3 minutes.

-Add all remaining ingredients, except raisins, peanut butter, and cilantro. Bring to a boil. Reduce heat to low and simmer, covered, for 20 minutes.

-Stir in raisins, peanut butter, and cilantro. Mix well. Simmer for 5 minutes. Serve hot over rice or grain of choice.

Number of Servings: 8

Vegan Chili

Ingredients:

4 cans of tomato sauce

1 can of pinto beans

1 onion cubed

1 package of meatless ground crumbles

1 small square of cocoa chocolate

2 tablespoons of chili powder

1 tablespoon of black pepper

½ teaspoon cinnamon

1/2 teaspoon nutmeg

Directions:

-In a non stick pan sauté the meatless ground crumbles and the diced onion until onion is soft.

-Combine all ingredients in a slow cooker and cook on high for 3 hours, and then switch to low until ready to eat.

Number of Servings: 10

Vegan Spinach and Ricotta Stuffed Manicotti

Ingredients:

1 lb firm tofu

1 10 oz frozen spinach (thawed)

1 tablespoon garlic powder

1/4 cup nutritional yeast

1 teaspoon salt and pepper

1 teaspoon oregano

3 or 4 tablespoons of olive oil

1 cup of mushrooms

1 package manicotti

1 vegan mozzarella soy block- grated

1 jar of spaghetti sauce

Directions:

-Drain the tofu for about 30 minutes before starting this recipe

-Squeeze thawed spinach by hand making sure it is not totally dry.

-Place all ingredients (except for the sauce) into a food processor. Pulse until well mixed and smooth. Take a taste and adjust your seasoning.

-Fill large bag with the mixture. Cut a dime size hole in bottom corner of bag. Pipe the filling into the tubes of manicotti filling them completely. Pour sauce into a large bowl. Fill up jar with about 1/2 cup of water and replace lid and shake. Add to sauce in bowl. Mix well and add some olive oil.

-Ladle half of sauce into a rectangular pan. Place stuffed manicotti into sauce. Top with remaining sauce. Cover with foil and bake for 20-25 minutes. Remove cover and top with vegan mozzarella and bake for another 10-15 minutes till bubbly. Let it cool and enjoy.

Number of Servings: 4

Vegan Sloppy Joes

Ingredients:

1 cup sweet onion, chopped

1 red bell pepper, chopped

1 cup mushrooms, sliced and chopped

3 cloves garlic, minced or chopped

2 tablespoons olive oil

1 10 oz package frozen spinach (the chopped kind)

1 can tomato paste (6oz)

6 tablespoons of steak sauce (A1 works best)

1 tablespoon dried parsley (or fresh if you like)

fresh ground pepper to taste

Directions:

-Take out spinach and set on counter to thaw (or run tap water over the package for a bit) while preparing the rest of the veggies.

-Rehydrate the TVP per package instructions.

-Heat olive oil over medium heat and sauté the onions first, until soft.

-Add peppers, sauté until tender.

-Add the mushrooms and garlic.

-Sautee for an additional 3-5 minutes until tender and blended well.

-Add slightly thawed spinach and cover for 3 minutes.

-Add can of tomato paste, stirring and mixing it in to the veggies. Cover for 2 minutes.

-Add A1 sauce and dried parsley

-Add rehydrated TVP and stir well. Cover for additional 10-15 minutes, stirring occasionally.

Serve with buns of your choice!

Number of Servings: 6-8

Vegan Jambalaya

Ingredients:

3 tablespoons olive oil

1 onion, coarsely chopped

1 bell pepper, coarsely chopped

3 tablespoons whole wheat flour

1 teaspoon minced garlic

1 14oz can vegetable broth

3/4 cup water

1 can diced tomatoes w/garlic, basil & oregano

1 can goya blackeye peas

1 cup long grain white rice (cooked)

1 teaspoon cayenne pepper

Seasoning to taste

Directions:

(Cook dry rice in a rice cooker while the rest of the ingredients are being cooked)

-In a stockpot, heat oil over medium heat. Add onion and pepper, stirring until softened, about 4-5 minutes. Stir in the flour and reduce the heat to medium-low. Cook until the flour turns brownish (if you're using wheat flour, 8 minutes should suffice). Add the garlic and cook one more minute.

Next, slowly add the broth and the water. Add the tomatoes with juice, blackeye peas, cooked rice, cayenne pepper, and creole seasoning.

-Bring to a boil, stirring from the bottom (if you don't stir the bottom, the rice will stick and burn).

-Reduce heat, cover and let simmer for 15 minutes or until the rice is tender.

Servings: 6

Vegan Spanish Casserole

Ingredients:

Olive oil for frying

1 cup each of 3 different types of beans (eg - Chickpeas, Pinto and Red Kidney)

1/2 a large onion

3 cloves garlic, chopped

1 cup red bell peppers, thinly sliced

10 pitted black olives, chopped

2 tins tomatoes

2 table spoon tomato puree

Half a teaspoon salt

Dash of soy sauce

Black pepper (to taste)

Basil (to taste)

1 Bay Leaf

Directions:

-In a large saucepan add the olive oil, garlic and fry the onion.

-Next, Add the Peppers and Olives. Fry for 5 mins stirring all the time

-Next, add all of the Beans. Cook for a further 10 mins stirring now and again to make sure the Beans don't stick to the bottom of the pan.

-Add the tins of tomatoes, the tomato paste, salt, soy sauce and bay leaf and place a lid over the saucepan. Simmer on a low heat for an hour to an hour and a half, stirring every 10 mins or so.

-10 mins before cooking time is finished add some chopped fresh Basil.

-Serve with warm crusty bread.

Number of Servings: 6

Vegan Stuffed Bell Peppers

Ingredients:

6 peppers (2 of each colour is nice)

1 can of tomato sauce (2 cups)

1 large onion (chopped)

2 cups of mushrooms

1 bunch of fresh spinach (not frozen)

2 cloves of garlic

2 tablespoons of fresh basil

1 jalapeno pepper

1 cup cooked brown rice

1/2 cup of shredded tempeh

Soy sauce to taste

Directions:

-Chop all the ingredients except the bell peppers because you need these so you can stuff them.

-Put all the ingredients in a large pot and add olive oil, garlic cloves (crushed), fresh basil, jalapeno and onions then cook on high for 3 minutes.

-Add the mushrooms (sliced) and tempeh (shredded) and simmer on medium heat for 5 minutes.

-Add the spinach and the rice and cover the pan and turn off the heat. This blends the flavors.

-Cut the tops off of the peppers and place to the side so you don't get them dirty. Keep the tops - don't throw them away as you need them.

-With a spoon, scoop out the seeds from the inside

-Fill the peppers with the mixture and place the tops back on them.

-Put peppers in a lightly oiled casserole dish and place in a preheated oven which has been heated to 350 degrees.

-Bake until the peppers are soft (about 15 minutes). Use a fork to check if they are soft.

Serving Size: 6

Vegan Shepherd's Pie

Ingredients:

2 cups of ground veggie beef

3cups frozen mixed veggies (slightly thawed)

1 package of instant gravy mix

4-5 large potatoes

1/2 cup soy milk

Directions:

-Peel & cut potatoes into small pieces, and place in a pot of boiling water.

-Cook until mushy, then mash the potatoes with the soy milk.

-In a baking dish, mix the ground veggie beef with the package of gravy, and about 1/2 cup hot water, then even out the veggie beef so it covers the bottom of the pan.

-Next add the veggies, and even them out.

-Top with the mashed potatoes.

-Bake for 30 minutes to 1 hour, covered, then remove cover and broil for 5 minutes to get a nice golden brown top.

Number of Servings: 6

DESSERTS

Vegan Apple Crisp

Ingredients:

-5 cups apples, thinly sliced, peeled if desired

-3/4 cup brown sugar (use a vegan one, not processed through bone char)

-3/4 cup whole wheat pastry flour

-3/4 cup old fashioned oats

-1 teaspoon cinnamon (generous)

-1/2 teaspoon nutmeg

-3 -4 tablespoons safflower oil

-2 tablespoons soymilk (or 2 tablespoons other non-dairy milk)

Directions:

-Preheat oven to 350.

-Mix the other ingredients, with a spoon, then with fingers, until the texture is crumbly. If too dry, add more oil or soymilk; if too wet, add more flour.

-Transfer the apples to a medium casserole or pie dish. Sprinkle the dry mixture over them and even it out a bit with a spoon.

-Bake for 1/2 hour, checking occasionally, till golden and crispy. Allow to cool a little before serving

Number of Servings: 6

Dark Chocolate Mousse

Ingredients:

2 large avocados, cubed (about 2 cups)

1/2 cup maple syrup

2 tablespoons coconut oil

2-4 tablespoons of organic or granulated sugar

Splash of water

1-2 tablespoons vanilla extract

1 teaspoon balsamic vinegar

1/2 teaspoon low-sodium soy sauce

1 cup cocoa powder (un-sweetened)

Directions:

-Add all ingredients except Cocoa Powder into a food processor or blender, pulse until smooth.

-Add Cocoa Powder to Avocado mixture and blend until smooth. (Add water if its too thick for the blender to mix)

-Taste, and add more sugar if too bitter and blend.

-Refrigerate in a tightly sealed container for up to a week.

-Serve with cool whip and your favorite berries

Number of Servings: 8

Vegan Soft Sugar Cookies

Ingredients:

3 tablespoons extra-firm silken tofu (mashed with a fork or pureed in processor or blender)

1/2 cup vegan margarine

1 teaspoon vanilla

1/2 cup sugar

1 1/4 cups flour

1 teaspoon baking powder

1/4 teaspoon salt

Directions:

-Cream margarine and sugar for about 5 minutes until fluffy.

-Add mashed tofu and vanilla. Mix well.

-Sift the flour, baking powder and salt into the mixture.

-You can either roll out the dough and use cookie cutters or make cookie dough balls and flatten the dough with your hand onto an ungreased cookie sheet

-Bake for around 10 mins in 350 degree oven.

-Note: You might need to adjust the flour a bit if the dough feels too wet. Also, these cookies aren't super sweet. If you like them that way, or if you aren't frosting them, you might want to add 2 more tablespoons sugar.

Number of Servings: 12

Vegan Brownies

Ingredients:

1 cup unsweetened applesauce

1/2 cup sugar

1 teaspoon vanilla

3/4 cup unbleached white flour

1/3 cup cocoa powder

2 teaspoons baking powder

1/2 teaspoon baking soda

1/2 teaspoon salt

1/2 cup semisweet vegan chocolate chips

1/3 cup walnuts (optional)

1 dash cinnamon (optional)

Directions:

-Preheat oven to 350 and lightly spray or oil an 8 x 8 baking pan.

-Mix applesauce, sugar, and vanilla in a medium bowl. In another bowl, whisk flour, cocoa, baking powder, baking soda, and salt (and cinnamon if using) together.

-Make a well in the center of the dry ingredients and add the applesauce mixture. -Mix until just combined. Gently fold in chocolate chips (and walnuts if using).

-Spread in prepared pan and bake 25-30 min, until center is firm and not sticky. Cool completely before slicing.

Number of Servings: 12

Vegan Banana Frosting

Ingredients:

1 banana

1/8 cup almond milk, (almond breeze unsweetened original)

1/2 cup brown sugar

1/2 teaspoon cornstarch

2 tablespoons flour, white

Directions:

-Peel banana and place in a medium bowl. Microwave for about 20 seconds.

-Mash banana and add all other ingredients.

-Beat with mixer until all is mixed well.

-Preparation time: 10 minutes or less

Number of Servings: Frosting for one cake

Vegan + Whole Wheat Scones

Ingredients:

2 cups whole wheat flour, plus extra for dusting

1/4 cup raw/turbinado sugar (plus 2 tablespoons to sprinkle on top)

1 teaspoon baking powder

1/4 teaspoon baking soda

1/2 teaspoon salt

1/2 cup Earth Balance margarine

1/4 cup soy or rice milk (unsweetened)

Directions:

-Preheat the oven to 400F.

-Mix dry ingredients together, making sure there are no lumps in your baking soda or baking powder.

-Rub in Earth Balance with your fingertips until the dough has a crumb like texture.

-Pour in the soymilk a little bit at a time, mixing as you go. You only need to add enough soymilk for the dough to stick together.

-Dust your countertop (or a large cutting board) with flour, and drop the dough onto the floured surface. Sprinkle a little more flour on top and form the dough into a circle about 1.5 inches thick. Cut the circle into 8 triangular slices like pie wedges.

-Place the scones onto a cookie sheet at least an inch apart. Sprinkle tops with additional sugar.

-Bake for 15-20 minutes, until golden on top and a toothpick inserted in the center comes out clean.

Number of Servings: 8

Vegan Chocolate Applesauce Cake

Ingredients:

2 cups flour

1 cup sugar

1 tablespoon cornstarch

2 teaspoons baking soda

1/4 teaspoon salt

1/3 cup cocoa powder, unsweetened

1 1/2 cups applesauce, unsweetened

Directions:

-Grease and flour 11x7 pan.

-Mix all of the dry ingredients in a large bowl.

-Add applesauce and mix well until batter is smooth.

-Bake for 50-55 minutes or until done. (Insert toothpick in center of cake; if comes out clean, cake is done.)

-Frost if desired.

Number of Servings: 10

Vegan Chocolate Fruit Balls

Ingredients:

1 cup nuts raw almonds, cashews, macadamias

1/2 cup organic pitted chopped dates

1/2 cup dried chopped apricot

1/2 cup raisins

2 tablespoons unsweetened cocoa powder

1 tablespoon fresh orange juice

2 drops of natural almond essence

1/2 teaspoon cinnamon

1/4 cup desiccated coconut

Directions:

-Mix the coconut and cinnamon in a small bowl and set aside for rolling.

-Put all other ingredients in a food processor, and slowly add in the orange juice if it doesn't bind together completely.

-Roll into small balls and coat with the coconut mixture.

-Store in a sealed glass container in the fridge.

Number of Servings: 15-20

Vegan Banana Peanut Butter Brownies

Ingredients:

4 bananas, fresh and mashed

1 tablespoon of natural peanut butter

1/2 cup Silk soymilk, light chocolate

1 cup of white flower

1/4 cup of powdered sugar, unsifted

1/2 cup of brown sugar, unpacked

1 teaspoon baking powder

1/2 teaspoon of salt

1/3 cups of cocoa, dry powder, unsweetened

Directions:

-Blend all till very smooth in a large bowl with a hand blender.

-Spray 9" x 9" baking pan with cooking spray and pour in batter.

-Bake at 350 for 30-35 min.

-Serve chilled.

Number of Servings: 9

Vegan Mixed Berry Muffins (Fat Free and Low Calorie!)

Ingredients:

1 ¾ cup flour (white)

4 teaspoons raw sugar

2 teaspoons Baking Powder

½ teaspoon of salt

1 ¼ cup 'trim' Soymilk

1 serving of Egg Replacer

25 grams applesauce (unsweetened)

½ cup Strawberries, frozen, (unsweetened)

¼ cup Blueberries, frozen (unsweetened)

¼ cup Blackberries, frozen (unsweetened) ¼ cup Raspberries, frozen (unsweetened)

Directions:

-Preheat oven to 400 degrees. Spray a 12-cup muffin tin with non-fat cooking spray.

-In a large bowl, combine all dry ingredients.

-In a smaller bowl- combine applesauce and soy milk.

-Chop the frozen berries into a manageable size

-Add wet ingredients to the dry, and stir to combine, adding berries as you mix

-Using a 1/4 cup measure, scoop into prepared muffin tin (they should be about 2/3 full), bake for 20-25 minutes (when a toothpick inserted comes out clean).

-Cool in tin for 5 minutes, and then turn out to cooling rack

-Serve warm.

Number of Servings: 12

Vegan Cinnamon Raisin Muffins (Whole Wheat!)

Ingredients:

1 cup whole wheat flour

1 teaspoon baking soda

1/2 teaspoon ground cinnamon

1/4 cup brown sugar

1/2 cup water

1/2 cup unsweetened applesauce

1/4 cup raisins

Directions:

-Line a muffin tray with 12 muffin cups, and spray each with non-stick cooking spray.

-Preheat oven to 350 degrees Fahrenheit.

-Mix whole wheat flour, baking soda, and ground cinnamon in a bowl. Add in brown sugar, water, and unsweetened applesauce, and stir the mixture until the ingredients are well blended.

-Spoon mixture evenly into 12 muffin cups. Bake for approximately 10 to 15 minutes, until muffin tops are golden.

Number of Servings: 12

Vegan Raisin Rice Pudding

Ingredients:

2 cups Light Soy Milk

2 cups Brown Rice (cooked)

2 teaspoon Cinnamon

1 tablespoon Vanilla

1 cup Raisins (not packed)

1/4 cup sweetener (Splenda)

Directions:

-In a medium saucepan combine everything and bring to a boil.

-Reduce heat and simmer on low for 15-20 minutes until pudding thickens to desired consistency, stirring occasionally.

Number of Servings: 4

Vegan Pumpkin Pancakes

Ingredients:

2 1/2 cups whole wheat flour

2 1/2 cups water

1/2 cup soy milk

2 tablespoons baking powder

1 teaspoon salt

1/2 cup mashed, cooked pumpkin

1/2 teaspoon cinnamon

1/4 teaspoon nutmeg

1/4 teaspoon allspice

1 teaspoon vanilla extract

1/2 teaspoon baking soda

1 teaspoon apple cider vinegar (or white if necessary)

Directions:

-Combine soymilk with the tsp vinegar in a separate bowl. Give it 5 minutes to curdle.

-Stir together pumpkin, spices, water and soymilk in mixing bowl. Add in remaining ingredients and stir until moist (no longer).

-Let sit 5 minutes to rise and lightly stir again. Let rest 5 more minutes and cook them up

Number of Servings: 20 small pancakes

Vegan Chocolate Almond Pudding

Directions:

3 tablespoons corn starch

3 tablespoons granulated sugar

2 tablespoons cocoa powder

2 cups unsweetened almond breeze original

1 teaspoon vanilla extract

Ingredients:

-Mix dry ingredients together and place in a blender along with the 2 cups of Almond Breeze.
-Blend well, and pour into a medium saucepan.
-Heat on medium, stirring occasionally until the mixture comes to a boil. Then reduce heat to a simmer and stir continuously for 4 or 5 minutes.
-Remove from heat, stir in 1 teaspoon of vanilla extract.
-Pour into four individual serving bowls or ramekins.
-Chill until set.
Number of Servings: 4

Vegan Banana Bread

Ingredients:

3 bananas

2 cups flour

dash of salt

1 teaspoon baking powder

3/4 cup sugar

2 tablespoon oil

Directions:

-Preheat the oven to 350*F.

-Mist a loaf pan with oil.

-In a large bowl, mash the 3 bananas with a fork until mostly smooth.

-Add oil, and mix thoroughly.

-Add baking powder and dash of salt to the mixture, and stir.

-Add flour and stir until combined.

-Pour batter into the loaf pan.

-Bake for 40 minutes, or until top is lightly golden and toothpick inserted in center comes out clean.

Number of servings: 10

Vegan Popsicles: Chocolate Peanut Butter Banana

Ingredients:

7 small bananas

2 teaspoon cocoa

1/4 cup peanut butter

14 popsicle sticks

Directions:

-Peel and cut bananas it half. Put a Popsicle stick in each half.

-Melt peanut butter in the microwave for 1 minute, on half power.

 -Mix in cocoa with the peanut butter.

-Get a brush and brush the mixture on all sides of each banana. Place on parchment paper

-Freeze for at least an hour.

Optional: Roll them in chocolate chips or chopped nuts after adding the peanut butter glaze.

Serving Size: 14

Vegan Pumpkin Bars

Ingredients:

2 cups all-purpose flour

3/4 cup Splenda Blend for Baking

3 teaspoons ground cinnamon

2 teaspoons baking powder

1-1/2 teaspoons ground cloves

1 teaspoon baking soda

1/4 teaspoons salt

8 tablespoons finely ground flax seed

12 tablespoons water

15 oz pumpkin

1 cup unsweetened applesauce

Directions:

-Mix flour, Splenda, spices, baking powder, baking soda and salt together in a large bowl.

-Add the water to the ground flax seed to make a thin paste.

-Add flax seed paste, pumpkin, and applesauce to dry ingredients and mix until smooth.

-Pour batter into an ungreased 15x9x1 baking pan and bake at 350 degrees for 25 minutes or until toothpick inserted into center comes out clean.

-Cool on wire rack and cut into bars.

Number of Servings: 24

Vegan Coffee Cake (Low-Fat)

Ingredients:

1/4 cup margarine

2 cups applesauce

1 cup flour

1 1/2 cups wheat bran flakes or oat bran

1 cup sugar

1 teaspoon baking soda

1 teaspoon cinnamon

1/2 teaspoon nutmeg

1/4 teaspoon cloves

1 cup raisins

Directions:

-Pre-heat oven to 350 degrees and grease the bottom of a 9-inch square baking pan.

-In a large saucepan, heat the margarine and applesauce together until margarine is melted. Remove from heat.

-Add the remaining ingredients and mix until well combined, then pour into baking pan.

-Bake for 25-30 minutes, until a toothpick inserted in the center comes out clean.

Number of Servings: 9

Vegan Double Chocolate Chip Cookies

Ingredients:

1/2 cup canola oil

1 cup sugar

1 tablespoon vanilla

1 tablespoon ground flax seeds

1/2 cup soy milk

1 1/2 cups all-purpose flour

3/4 cup dutch processed cocoa powder

1 teaspoon baking soda

1/2 teaspoon salt

1 cup vegan chocolate chips

Directions:

-In a large bowl, sift together flour, cocoa, baking soda and salt.

-In a separate large bowl cream together oil and sugar. Add the flax seeds and soy milk. Mix well. Add the vanilla.

-Fold in the dry ingredients in small batches. Add the chocolate chips.

-Roll dough into 1 inch balls and place on a greased cookie sheet (you could also use parchment paper here) about an inch apart. The cookies will not spread out that much.

-Bake for 10 minutes at 350 F.

-Remove from oven and let cool for about 5 minutes, then set them on a wire rack to cool completely.

Number of Servings: 36

Vegan Donuts

Ingredients:

2 cups flour

1/2 cup vegan sugar

2 teaspoons baking powder

1 1/2 teaspoons egg substitute

2 tablespoons water

3/4 cup rice milk

1 teaspoon vanilla extract

4 teaspoons oil

Directions:

-Preheat oven to 325 degrees.

-Mix flour, sugar, and baking powder.

-Add egg replacer + water (mixed together before adding), rice milk, oil, and vanilla, mix vigorously until well blended.

-Pour batter into a doughnut pan

-Put in oven and bake for 8-10 minutes or until done.

-Dip into a mixed sugar glaze (powdered sugar and water) or roll in a bag filled with cinnamon and sugar.

Number of Servings: 18 donuts

Vegan Peanut Butter Cookies

Ingredients:

1/2 cup apple sauce

3/4 cup peanut butter

1 teaspoon vanilla

1 1/4 cup brown sugar

1 cup whole wheat pastry flour

3/4 cup unbleached flour

3/4 teaspoon baking soda

3/4 teaspoon salt

Directions:

-Preheat oven to 375.

-Mix the apple sauce, peanut butter and vanilla together. Add the brown sugar. Add soda and salt to the flour and gradually add the flour mixture to the creamed ingredients.

-Drop tablespoon-sized dough balls onto cookie sheet and press down in classic fork pattern.

-Bake for 10-12 minutes, depending on how you like them

-Adding chocolate chips is optional

Number of Servings: 2

Vegan Banana Muffins

Ingredients:

3 mashed bananas

1 cup sugar

1/4 cup vegetable oil

2 cups flour

1 teaspoons salt

1 teaspoons baking soda

Cinnamon or Nutmeg to sprinkle on top (if desired mixed with brown sugar or margarine)

Directions:

-Mix mashed bananas, sugar and oil.

-Add in dry ingredients.

-Bake at 360*F 15-18 minutes.

Number of Servings: 24

Vegan Vanilla Cupcakes

Ingredients:

1 cup soy milk

1 teaspoon apple cider vinegar

1 1/4 cup all-purpose flour

2 tablespoons cornstarch

3/4 teaspoon baking powder

1/2 teaspoon baking soda

1/2 teaspoon salt

1/3 cup canola oil

3/4 cup granulated sugar

2 1/4 teaspoon pure vanilla extract

Directions:

-Preheat oven to 350 F

-Whisk vinegar into soy milk and set aside to curdle (consistency of buttermilk.)

-Sift flour, cornstarch, baking powder and soda, and salt in a small bowl. Mix well.

-In a separate bowl beat together soymilk, oil, sugar, vanilla until frothy.

-Beat dry ingredients into wet ingredients until well mixed and no lumps

-Fill cupcake liners 2/3 to 3/4 full.

-Bake for 18-20 or until an inserted toothpick comes out clean.

-Transfer to cooling rack until completely cooled and frost with vegan buttercream frosting.

Number of Servings: 12 cupcakes

Vegan Apple Carrot Muffins

Ingredients:

2 cup unsweetened soy milk

1/2 cup brown sugar

1/4 cup applesauce, unsweetened

1 tablespoon canola oil

2 1/2 cup whole wheat pastry flour

4 teaspoons baking powder

1 teaspoon ground cinnamon

1/4 teaspoon salt

1/2 cup grated carrot

1 medium apple, chopped small

Directions:

-Prepare muffin tins with nonstick spray. Preheat oven to 350 degrees.

-In a medium bowl, mix soymilk, brown sugar, applesauce, and canola oil.

-In another bowl, mix dry ingredients. Add liquid to dry, scraping the bottom to get any brown sugar residue. Stir to combine. Add carrots and apples.

-Pour into muffin cups.

-Bake for 15 minutes or until muffins are golden.

Vegan Zucchini Banana Muffins (Whole Wheat!)

Ingredients:

2 1/2 tablespoons ground flax seed mixed with 1/2 cup + 1 tablespoon water

3 1/2 cups shredded zucchini (about 2 medium zucchinis)

3 bananas, mashed

1 tablespoon vanilla

1 cup sugar

2 cups unbleached white flour

2 cups whole wheat flour

1/2 cup wheat germ

1 teaspoon salt

1 1/2 teaspoons baking soda

1 1/2 teaspoons baking powder

1 1/2 teaspoons ground cloves or nutmeg

2 tablespoons cinnamon

Directions:

-Preheat oven to 350 degrees. Lightly grease two loaf pans or two muffin tins (24 muffins total) or use cupcake liners, set aside.

-Combine ground flax and water, set aside. In large bowl, combine zucchini, bananas, sugar and vanilla. Add flax mixture. In medium bowl, combine dry ingredients. Add to wet ingredients in 2-3 batches. Mix until completely combined.

-Divide equally into loaf pans (or muffin tins).

    -Bake muffins for 15-20 minutes.

    -Bake bread for 35-45 minutes.

-Use toothpick test for doneness.

These will freeze well.

Number of Servings: 24 muffins or two loafs

Vegan Fruit-Butter Bars

Ingredients:

1 1/2 cups whole wheat pastry flour

1 1/2 cups quick-cooking rolled oats (not instant)

1/4 cup unbleached cane sugar

1/2 teaspoon baking soda

1/4 teaspoon salt

1/2 cup maple syrup

1/4 cup canola oil

1 1/2 cups thick fruit butter (apple, pumpkin, prune or peach)

Directions:

-Preheat oven to 350 degrees.

-Lightly oil or spray sides and bottom of a glass baking pan, 8 inches square and 2 inches deep.

-To make the crust, place the flour, oats, sugar, baking soda and salt in a large mixing bowl and stir them together until well combined.

-In a small mixing bowl, stir together the maple syrup and oil. Pour into the flour-oat mixture and mix thoroughly until everything is evenly moistened. The mixture will be crumbly.

-Press half of this mixture evenly into prepared baking pan, packing it down very firmly.

-Carefully spread the fruit butter evenly over the base. Sprinkle the rest of the flour-oat mixture evenly over the fruit butter and pat down lightly.

Bake for 20 to 25 minutes, or until lightly brown. Cool on a wire rack and slice into bars or squares.

Number of Servings: 4

Vegan Chocolate Cupcakes

Ingredients:

1 cup soy milk

1 teaspoon apple cider vinegar

3/4 cup granulated sugar

1/3 cup canola oil

1 teaspoon vanilla extract

1/2 teaspoon almond extract, chocolate extract, or more vanilla extract

1 cup all-purpose flour

1/3 cup cocoa powder

3/4 teaspoon baking soda

1/2 teaspoon baking powder

1/4 teaspoon salt

Directions:

-Preheat oven to 350°F and line a muffin pan with paper or foil liners.

-Whisk together the soy milk and vinegar in a large bowl, and set aside for a few minutes to curdle. Add the sugar, oil, vanilla extract, and other extract (if using) to the soy milk mixture and beat until foamy.

-In a separate bowl, sift together the flour, cocoa powder, baking soda, baking powder, and salt.

-Add in two batches to wet ingredients and beat until no large lumps remain

-Pour into liners, filling 3/4 of the way. Bake 18 to 20 minutes, until a toothpick inserted into the center comes out clean. Transfer to a cooling rack and let cool completely.

Number of Servings: 12 cupcakes

Vegan Blueberry Banana Muffins

Ingredients:

For the Muffins:

3 ripe bananas

1/4 cup vegetable oil

1 cup sugar

1 teaspoon salt

1 teaspoon baking soda

2 cups flour, divided

3/4 cup fresh or unthawed frozen blueberries

For the Crumb Topping:

1/2 cup flour

1/2 cup brown sugar

4 tablespoons non-dairy margarine

Directions:

-Preheat the oven to 350°F.

-In a medium bowl, mash the bananas with the oil and sugar and mix well.

-In a small bowl, sift together the salt, baking soda, and 2 cups of the flour.

-Add the dry mixture to the banana mixture and stir by hand until the two are thoroughly combined. Fold in the blueberries.

-Pour the batter into a lined muffin pan.

-In a small bowl, combine the remaining 1/2 cup of flour, the brown sugar, and the non-dairy margarine. Stir until the mixture forms coarse crumbs then sprinkle the crumbs onto the muffins.

-Bake the muffins for 25 minutes or until a toothpick inserted in the middle comes out clean.

Number of Servings: 10-12 Muffins

Vegan Pumpkin Oatmeal Cookies

Ingredients:

2 cups flour

1 1/3 cups rolled oats

1 teaspoon baking soda

3/4 teaspoon salt

1 tsp cinnamon

1/2 teaspoon nutmeg

1 2/3 cups sugar

2/3 cup canola oil

2 tablespoons brown sugar

1 cup canned pumpkin, or cooked pureed pumpkin

1 teaspoon vanilla

3/4 cup vegan chocolate chips

Directions:

-Preheat oven to 350. Grease or line two baking sheets, set aside.

-In a medium bowl, combine flour, oats, baking soda, salt, cinnamon and nutmeg. Set aside.

-In a large bowl, combine sugars, oil, pumpkin and vanilla. Add dry ingredients in batches, folding to combine. Add the chocolate chips, folding to combine.

-Drop batter by spoonfuls onto cookie sheets about one inch apart. Bake for 15 minutes, longer if you want a firmer cookie. Let cool on a wire rack or plate in a single layer.

Number of Servings: 32 (individual cookies)

Vegan Banana Crumble

Ingredients:

For the filling:

4 medium bananas (ripe and sliced in round discs)

1/2 cup granulated sugar

For the crumble:

1/2 cup quick-cooking oats

1/2 cup whole wheat pastry flour or 1/2 cup unbleached flour

1/2 cup firmly packed brown sugar

1/2 cup vegan margarine (earth balance)

1/2 cup shredded unsweetened coconut (toasted)

1/4 teaspoon nutmeg, fresh ground or 1/4 teaspoon cinnamon if you wish

Directions:

-Preheat your oven to 350'F.

-Lightly oil 12 individual ramekins or one 9 inch square or round pan.

-Peel the bananas and slice them, then add to a bowl and add the sugar, give it a gentle mix to coat the banana and set aside.

-To make the crumble melt the earth balance margarine, set aside. Mix the oats, flour, brown sugar, coconut and butter together. Mix well so that all the dry ingredients are coated with the earth balance.

-Put your banana into the pan covering the bottom completely with banana. Add the crumble topping and sprinkle a little nutmeg on top.

-Bake for about 20 minutes or until bubbly.

-Serve warm or at room temperature.

Number of Servings: 6

Vegan Fudge

Ingredients:

4 cup powdered sugar

1/2 cup cocoa

1/2 cup soy milk

2 tablespoons of earth balance margarine

1 1/2 teaspoons vanilla

1 cup marshmallows

1/2 cup chopped nuts

Directions:

-Spray a 9x9 inch pan with cooking spray

-Sift sugar and cocoa together, then add the chocolate chips and set aside.

-In a small sauce pan, heat soy milk and butter together until they achieve a rolling boil; be sure to stir constantly.

-Pour over sugar mixture and stir until well combined.

-Stir in vanilla, marshmallows and nuts. Spread in pan and refrigerate for one day so that it solidifies well.

Number of Servings: 16 pieces

Vegan Breakfast Cookies

Ingredients:

1 1/3 cup cups oats

4 tablespoons raisins

4 tablespoons flour

1 1/3 cups powdered soy milk

1 cup unsweetened applesauce (no-sugar-added)

1 teaspoon cinnamon

1 teaspoon baking powder

4 tablespoon no-calorie artificial sweetener

Directions:

-Preheat oven to 350 degrees.

-Spray a large cookie sheet with Pam or use two smaller cookie sheets.

-Mix all ingredients together and spoon on sheet.

-Bake for 15-20 minute.

Number of Servings: 6

Vegan Whole Wheat Waffles

Ingredients:

1 cup whole wheat flour

3/4 teaspoon baking powder

Pinch of sea salt

3 tablespoons sugar

1/4 teaspoon cinnamon

1 cup soy milk

2 tablespoons vegetable oil

Directions:

-Mix dry ingredients together in a large mixing bowl. Gently stir in soy milk and oil. Prepare according to waffle iron instructions.

Variations: add in chopped nuts or some very small diced fruits.

Serving size: 8 small waffles

Vegan Oatmeal Pancakes

Ingredients:

1 cup flour

1/2 cup quick oatmeal (not instant)

1 tablespoon sugar

1/2 teaspoon cinnamon

1/2 teaspoon salt

1/2 teaspoon baking powder

1/2 teaspoon baking soda

1 tablespoon canola oil

1 tablespoon lemon juice (or vinegar)

1-1/4 cups soy milk

Directions:

-Put 1 tablespoon of lemon juice (or vinegar) in a 1 cup measure and fill cup with soy milk. Set aside.

-Measure all of the dry ingredients into a bowl and mix together with a spoon.

-Pour in the oil, and the soured soy milk. Stir until just mixed. If not thin enough for pancake batter, stir in up to 1/4 cup more of soy milk (or water).

-Fry in margarine as for regular pancakes

-Serve with fresh sliced strawberries or with maple syrup and margarine.

Number of Servings: 10 pancakes

Vegan Chocolate Cake

Ingredients:

3 cups Flour

2 cups Sugar

2/3 cup sifted cocoa powder

2 teaspoons baking soda

1 teaspoon salt

2 cup water

2/3 cup vegetable oil

2 teaspoon white vinegar

1 teaspoon vanilla extract

Directions:

-Preheat oven to 350 degrees & spray pans with non-stick spray

-Whisk dry ingredients together thoroughly.

-Add wet ingredients and whisk until combined.

-Divide batter evenly between cake pans.

-Bake 30 - 35 minutes until a toothpick comes out with a few wet crumbs.

-Cool cakes in pans on wire racks for 10 minutes.

-Unmold cakes onto wire racks to cool completely.

Number of Servings: 16

Vegan Pumpkin Chocolate Chip Cookies

Ingredients:

1 ¾ cups of pumpkin (1 can)

1 cup granulated sugar

1/2 cup vegetable oil

1 cup applesauce

2 cups all purpose flour

2 teaspoons baking powder

2 teaspoons cinnamon

1/2 teaspoon salt

1 teaspoon baking soda

1 tablespoon vanilla

2 cups vegan chocolate chips

Directions:

-Preheat oven to 350 degrees.

-Combine pumpkin, sugar, vanilla, oil, and applesauce.

-Combine flour, baking powder, baking soda, cinnamon, salt and add to pumpkin mixture gradually. Mix well.

-Bake in oven for 12-15 mins or until light brown and firm.

Number of Servings: 48 small cookies

Vegan Ginger Snaps

Ingredients:

3 cups all-purpose flour

1 tablespoon ground ginger

1 teaspoon salt

1/2 cup applesauce

2 tablespoons oil

1/2 cup white sugar

1 cup molasses

Directions:

-Combine flour, ginger and salt and set aside.

-In a large bowl, mix oil, applesauce and sugar. Beat in the molasses. Gradually blend in the dry ingredients. Cover and chill for four hours.

-Preheat oven to 350 degrees F. Lightly grease cookie sheets.

-On floured surface, roll out dough to 1/4 inch thickness. Using a 1-3/4 inch cutter, cut into rounds and place 1 inch apart on cookie sheets.

-Bake for 10-12 minutes until lightly colored and firm to the touch. Cool cookies on wire racks.

Number of Servings: 18

Printed in Great Britain
by Amazon